Time In My Mind

Hope You Enjoy

Time In My Mind

James N. Bakker

To order additional copies of this book, contact:
Xlibris Corporation
1-888-795-4274
www.Xlibris.com
Orders@Xlibris.com
83603

Contents

James N. Bakker first started writing poetry at the age of fifteen years and continued writing through his earlier days, changing ideas as the years went by. Eventually, he began to write with more heart and soul inspiration, which is where the majority of his poetry began to excel.

Through time, he began to focus on everything that happened in his life and in those lives around him whether they were family, friends, or just everyday events.

"Through the mind, soul, and heart comes the true inspiration to create poetry."

"One can only express what the inner spirit will allow it to release."

James Bakker

A New Start

All is silent, all is still,
All is dark and calm until;
Sudden movement, sudden sound,
Wakes me up to look around.

There you sit so patiently,
Waiting calmly just for me;
As you noticed, as you knew,
I am anxious to help you.

In an instant when you call,
We head for the hospital;
As we arrive safely there,
We are ready to prepare.

Anxious moments, anxious dreams,
All come quickly, so it seems;
Through the pain, through the fear,
Finally arrives someone dear.

So excited, so relieved,
Such a blessing we received;
You are finally set free,
We've become a family.

Memories

Once again, I found myself sitting in my grandfather's meadow, marveling at the way the tall slender grass waved back and forth as the waves of the ocean. I remember how I used to come to this place when I was younger to ponder my joys and injustices. I glanced up at the sky, and as the warm reddish-orange sun waved a last good-bye before descending into the hillside, I thought about how content I had been here. Fond memories popped in and out of my mind about my first love and about how the fervent sunset beamed off her smiling face, creating a beauty unmatched by anyone I ever had seen before. I also recall how the warm southern breeze combined with her presence used to send shivers up my spine. I realized then that I had been more content with life here than any other place I had been before. There I sat pondering even more enlightenments when the air grew cool and all grew dark. The wind whistled around and the stars said good-bye as the cloud cover grew. Then thunder rumbled from above interrupting the peacefulness, which had been my hint to depart at least for now, until the next chance came to dream again, and I hoped it would be soon.

Passing Strength

All on your own you made life great,
With your soft smile you sealed my fate;
No one has been more worth the wait,
Than you, my love, my lifelong mate.

You touched my heart with words you said,
You had my mind at all times read;
Your love was food to keep me fed,
With you passing my joy has fled.

You once did say if you were gone,
That I should stay and face each dawn;
You'd remain by me my whole life long,
And in my mind you'd keep me strong.

With you away I can only cry,
If you were here you'd ask me why;
We both had said if we were to die,
Our soul wouldn't fall but reach the sky.

Our Lord in heaven has called you home,
For now I'll be subsequently along;
But soon my love we will meet again,
At the golden gate up in heaven.

Sensations

With my eyes I see the beauty,
And the wonder of this place;
The trees and hills surrounding me,
And sunset showing face.

With my nose I smell the beauty,
As the ocean draws up air;
While the breeze blows through the trees,
The scent's beyond compare.

With my ears I hear the beauty,
As the birds sing peacefully;
The crashing of the ocean tides,
Completes the serenity.

With my lips I taste the beauty,
Of fresh fruit hanging on trees;
And crystal clear water flows,
From nearby mountain streams.

With my face I feel the beauty,
As the warm air taps my skin;
I realize how blessed I must be,
To have these senses within.

An Exquisite Journey

It's a cool blue morning
The ground is white
The sun is shinning
And skies are bright.

The journey begins
With a flight to the coast
West over the mountains
The air as a host.

From one time to another
And one temperature too
Each place to arrive at
Presents something new.

And from that destination
To the next waiting by
You follow the journey
Taking to the sky.

You wave to the city
And the land disappears
Leaving ocean beneath
Until land re-appears.

Then out pours excitement
As you see the islands
And the beautiful beaches
Surrounded by white sands.

Once you make your landing
The enjoyment starts fast
But like any vacation
It does not always last.

Back on Track

I stand high above streets,
On a pleasant, clear night;
I wish I could stay,
But an end is in sight.

My mind, once a clutter,
Is refreshed and clear;
The stress has subsided,
Due to our visit here.

All the time we have shared,
Through a number of days;
Has been so much enjoyed,
In an abundance of ways.

With the clear, sunny skies,
And mild ocean tides;
The rest we've encountered,
Has renewed us inside.

As I feel the warm breeze,
And think of going back;
I'll be glad that this journey,
Has put me back on track.

Unusual Day

It was a usual lunch on a usual day;
My stomach growled in its usual way.
I answered its call as I usually do;
That's when I discovered you.

You were where you usually stood;
I ordered my usual food.
I acted cool as I usually act,
But when you spoke I couldn't react.

My heart pumped an unusual beat;
I felt dizzy on my feet.
Something unusual was happening;
My usual lunch suddenly took wing.

I ascended to past cloud nine,
In an unusually short time.
My usual lunch turned out quite strange,
And my life took an unusual change.

After about a month or two,
I asked to go out with you.
Through time we took things in stride,
Next thing I knew you were my bride.

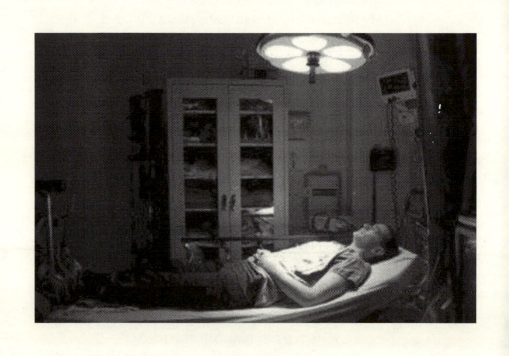

The Surgery Room

Here I lay waiting, with you next to me;
Wondering how long my wait will be.
My mind fills with fear like never before,
Because I'm unsure of what is in store.

You kiss me, then they roll me away;
And in the next room patiently I lay.
Then in come the nurses to prepare me,
For my delicate surgery.

They mask my face and ask me to breathe deep;
Then quickly there's darkness, as I fall fast asleep.
Within a few minutes I begin dreaming,
Of passing to a new life or so it would seem.

Then slowly my eyes open and the sting begins;
I feel it's my payback for all of my sins.
I ask for a sedative since the pain's so immense,
And when they reply it makes little sense.

There's a constant strain such as I've never felt,
Due to the situation that I have been dealt;
But sooner or later the discomfort will leave,
And I will be cured, this I surely believe.

My Inner Self

I feel my heart
Tear apart,
With the news each passing day brings;
And in my mind
I cannot find
Answers for such disturbing things.

It just may be
A sign for me,
To test my inner strength;
For with such news
I feel confused,
To an extended length.

Deep down inside
I try to hide,
But find no sheltering place;
Perhaps I must
Try to adjust
To these problems that I face.

Waking in Pain

Another painful awakening,
My head feels in a vice;
Anguish consumes my body,
Painkillers won't suffice.

The pain is so consistent,
Not wanting to cease;
I pray it will end quickly,
To put my mind at ease.

On top of my pillow,
All marked in red;
Rests my punished conscience,
That's medication fed.

First dreaming, then waking,
Over and over again;
I only feel the comfort,
Until I wake in pain.

And all the bitten places,
All around my tongue;
Add to the discomfort,
Of when the pain begun.

As the days pass onward,
Healing becomes complete;
Until the next awakening,
When everything repeats.

Part-time Bros

We are a family
Of a different kind;
We all join together
Each week to unwind.
We talk and drink coffee
To relax our minds,
And we catch up on news
To keep each day aligned.

We are not related,
Only real good friends;
When we join together
The fun never ends.
We know each other
Because no one pretends,
And any big problems,
We solve as good friends.

Day in and day out,
Our friendship grows;
And as for the reason
Each one of us knows.
If there's trouble among us,
We're on each other's toes;
It sure is a good thing
We remain PART-TIME BROS.

West Coast Dreams

I lay still in bed one night,
Sound asleep in much delight;
Dreaming of a place I'd been before,
A place that I so much adored.

Skies seemed always blue and clear,
With sunshine always to appear;
Scenery was arranged amazingly,
And in short drive was the sea.

It was a reminder of earlier days,
Which I enjoyed in so many ways;
So much to wake me up in the night,
And anxiously wait until daylight.

When I awoke early the next day,
I answered my dream's wish right away;
I decided to make my dream come true,
And off to the West Coast I flew.

Someone Special

As each day begins
With a rising sun;
Life has new meaning
Because of someone.

Someone so special,
Of which I am part;
That means so much to me,
Deep inside my heart.

Someone so wonderful,
More than I'd ever dream;
That's filled with purity,
To glow as it seems.

Someone who's my daughters,
My very joy and pride;
Who I will be part of,
The rest of my life.

Down by the Riverside

I stepped out of the house
And into the car;
Headed for a special place
That wasn't too far.
On my way to that spot
I stopped for some bait;
Then continued along
For my important date.

I arrived at the river
Sometime around dusk;
And got myself prepared
For a night so robust.
The sunshine vanished
And the wind died down;
Lights shined on the water,
Reflecting from the town.

I sat down and waited
Until about half past two;
Then it started to surface
As it tends to do.
A bell began ringing
Which startled us all;
And I rushed to my pole
Alert to someone's call.

Then came a strike,
And a good one at that;
After a long struggle,
There exhausted I sat.
Perhaps another time
We'd meet at the shore;
And I'd be the victor
As I'd never had before.

Determination

In a minute or two
You'll know what to do,
If you let me explain
Why I'm feeling this pain.

I want you to see
How good things can be,
If we both work together
Through this stormy weather.

There's just not enough space
In what seems a small place;
And we fail to grow closer
As we start to get older.

But if together we try
To do our best you and I,
To mend all our issues
We will show our love's true.

At this current rate
We may seal our fate,
And we might have to part
Breaking both of our hearts.

Rain, Rain, Rain Go Away

Rain, rain go away,
We don't want you here today;
We are tired of getting wet,
How much more wet will we get?

Rain, rain go away,
There's no need for you to stay;
The land out here has had its fill,
All this wet's making me ill.

Rain, rain go away,
Come back later if you may;
Waters now are getting high,
It's time for you to say good-bye.

Rain, rain go away,
You've had enough of your way;
I think it's time we see the sun,
With you here it is no fun.

My Buddy

I have a real good buddy,
Who's always there for me;
And every time I need him,
He's waiting patiently.

On every day my buddy,
Is anxious to go out;
And listens to what I will say,
Without having to shout.

Through the stormy weather,
No matter what it be;
I can always count on him,
To be there to protect me.

Like no other buddy,
His devotion never lacks;
I never need be insecure,
As he watches my back.

On the odd occasion,
My buddy might get ill;
I am always there for him,
To pay off his sick bill.

Weather Report

Again it is that time of day,
That unfortunately I must say;
The current weather will remain,
So sit right back enjoy the rain.

If you find it hard to take,
Start praying for a sunny break;
Perhaps by the time you are done,
You may enjoy a little sun.

In the meantime go to bed,
Dream of sunshine in your head;
Maybe when your sleeping's through,
The sun might be out to greet you.

Now you've awaken from you dreams;
The sun's not here or so it seems.
Please be patient wait and see,
It will come, believe you me.

Alas! I see the sun up high,
Shining bright in the blue sky.
Your prayers are answered finally;
Enjoy the time while it's sunny.

Changing "A" Life

A good friend asked me
When talking one day;
"How do you have a good time,
If you don't have the 'A?"

I smiled at him and answered
In my usual way;
"Life really isn't everything
If you have got the 'A.'"

He laughed and responded
With what I usually hear;
"That cannot be possible,
Without any 'A' near!"

I began to explain to him
Very explicitly;
"It isn't the 'A' you need,
Listen, and you'll see."

He gave me a puzzled look,
When I filled him in;
After thinking for a while,
He began to grin.

Now he realized how I felt,
But kept it to himself;
When engagements came along,
The "A" stayed on the shelf.

"A" Already

Whiskey Neighbor

The man who lives next door to us,
Does a large amount of drinking;
And when he exceeds his limit,
He does things without thinking.

For instance, just the other night,
He ended up quite drunk;
Somehow he locked himself into,
The inside of his car trunk.

Or late last night the other day,
He came home from the bar;
And just a half a block away,
He totaled off his car.

Many times he's been crazy,
Running out on the front lawn;
That would have never bothered us,
If he had any clothes on.

There's been an awful lot of things,
That through the years he's done.
They'll keep being a part of him,
Until the whiskey's gone.

Your Reward

Look at your neighbor
Whoever it may be,
And show them a smile
That they can see.
Ask them a question
Concerning Me;
Then tell them of the treasures
In My great treasury.

Expect many answers
That are somewhat stern;
Some that are thoughtless
Which like fire burn.
Whoever you comfort
I'm hoping you'll learn,
How to introduce Me
When it comes your turn.

Whatever happens
In your traveling days,
You will always be blessed
In so many ways;
Change one man in a thousand
To show Me praise;
And your reward will be given
At the end of your days.

Have You Ever Wondered?

Have you ever wondered,
Why heavy rain falls;
It is the Lord crying,
When we ignore His calls.

Have you ever wondered,
Why winds blow strong;
It's the Lord whispering to us,
That we should get along.

Have you ever wondered,
Why the earth trembles;
It's the Lord declaring,
We should heed to His calls.

Have you ever wondered,
Why it's a beautiful day;
It's God showing happiness,
In a weather-type way.

My Keeper

The Lord is my keeper
By night and by day;
He's always beside me
Whenever I stray.
He keeps and He guides me
Through sickness and health;
And having Him near me
Is my greatest wealth.

Forgiving and helpful
Is what He always is;
He constantly maintains
The love that He gives.
Naturally without Him
It would be hard to live;
It's so easy living
With the guidance He gives.

I will never be frightened
Because He's always near;
And whenever I call Him
He will always hear.
I know that without Him
My life would be gone;
He will never leave me
But only make me strong.

Give Me Strength

Give strength to me, Lord,
To continue to fight;
Give strength to me, Lord,
By day and by night.

Bring strength to me, Lord,
To get through the pain;
Bring strength to me, Lord,
For time in life to gain.

Grant strength to me, Lord,
To let go the stress;
Grant strength to me, Lord,
To outwardly confess.

Show strength to me, Lord,
To follow Your way;
Show strength to me, Lord,
Through every day.
Show strength to me, Lord,
In Your Word I pray.

Imagine

Imagine yourself walking,
Along a mountain path;
When a grizzly bear confronts you,
With affection and not wrath.

Imagine yourself swimming,
In ocean waters blue;
When a great white shark approaches,
And swims peacefully with you.

Imagine yourself resting,
In the hot desert sunlight;
When a scorpion climbs on you,
But decides not to bite.

Imagine yourself flying,
When skies turn dark and gray;
And though you're struck by lightning,
You safely make your way.

Imagine circumstances,
Such as all of these;
Someday one may confront you,
Of life's great mysteries.

Life's Highway

Life is one big highway,
Covering the earth;
And each lane on that highway,
Has its separate worth.

When you ride that highway,
Stay in the right lane;
For then you will surely assure,
You'll have so much to gain.

There are;
Lanes of love and lanes of hate,
Lanes of luck and lanes of fate;
Lanes of giving and lanes of greed,
Lanes of want and lanes of need.

There are;
Lanes of sickness, lanes of health,
Lanes of poverty, lanes of wealth;
Lanes of tension and lanes of ease,
Lanes of war and lanes of peace.

There are;
Lanes of right and lanes of wrong,
Lanes of weak and lanes of strong;
Lanes of fear, lanes of bold,
Lanes of young, lanes of old.

The Untouchables

With a stick in hand and blades on his feet,
He moves like scarce other beings;
The strides he takes, so smooth and unique,
Display him like few other men seen.

The movements he makes are so precise,
Mistakes are seldom recognized;
His talent makes everyone look twice,
Satisfaction on their faces abides.

Total control exists constantly,
Except the odd circumstances;
For anyone it's so easy to see,
How this man truly enhances.

He's an untouchable,
Unmarked, unbeaten, untouched;
He's an untouchable,
Unscathed by the wrath of others.
As 4, as 9, as 66, as 99 the untouchables;
He remains untouched.

Just as the stars up in the sky,
Eventually fade away;
This untouchable will pass by,
And another will take his place.

Freedom

I am a feather from a soaring eagle,
Floating freely in the wind;
High above the earth,
I follow my guide untouched.
I remain clean and pure,
And I am so free;
But will I remain untouched?
I could descend in an instant;
My guide is my stability,
And without it I will fall.
The feet of thousands will trample me;
Leaving me useless and without purpose,
But such is not the case.
I remain pure and simple,
Content with my freedom,
Upheld and free.

Enlightenment

There is always comfort,
In good things people say;
But comfort can leave them,
In one hardened phrase.

When you sense compassion,
You know something's right;
It's an inside sensation,
That opens new light.

There is often great power,
In friendship that's true;
Which will open a bond,
That will strengthen you.

With such a strong bond,
Will come true inner peace;
That will give enlightenment,
Setting your life at ease.

Weather Schemes

The cold winters days have ceased;
It is the time yet not the weather,
As the early warmth greets us.
Where has the white blanket gone?
We must be dreaming;
Is it not the cool airs' time?
Should we be content?
I certainly should think so.
Contentment has overcome me,
But will this contentment last?
Time will soon tell,
But for now all is warm,
Enlightening, and pleasant,
And we all know who to thank
For our blessing, or do we?

A Toy in Despair

I am a toy that sits on a shelf,
Brokenhearted and blue;
And cannot justify myself,
For I'm not used by you.

You are a child that always plays,
With toys that are brand new;
You save me for certain days,
When your friends visit you.

I sit around and collect dust,
From one day to another;
I cannot see why you must,
Save me for some other.

You don't realize what I am,
And never will unless;
You play with me some day again,
You may find happiness.

All I can do is sit and hope,
Some day you'll see me there;
For now I will just have to cope,
With being a toy in despair.

School Is Out

It was a fresh new day
When we went out to play;
The sun shone bright
Much to our delight.

School was all done
For each and everyone;
And now we had free time
With summer in its prime.

There was continuous joy
Among all girls and boys;
And in the fields nearby
We let our kites fly.

Unexplainable fun
Captured everyone;
As each day we were caught
By the relief summer brought.

Our minds loved to take
That summer time break;
But we knew in our hearts
Holidays would soon depart.

Spring Joy

I have taken time
To taste the sun,
And feel the warmth
That has finally come.

I have waved good-bye
To the cool breeze,
As falling rain
Will no longer freeze.

Once frozen streams
From cooler air,
Now freely flow
To who knows where.

The poplar trees
That have been empty,
Will soon have leaves
Showing their beauty.

The fine fresh scent
Of pine around,
Makes my heart lift
Up off the ground.

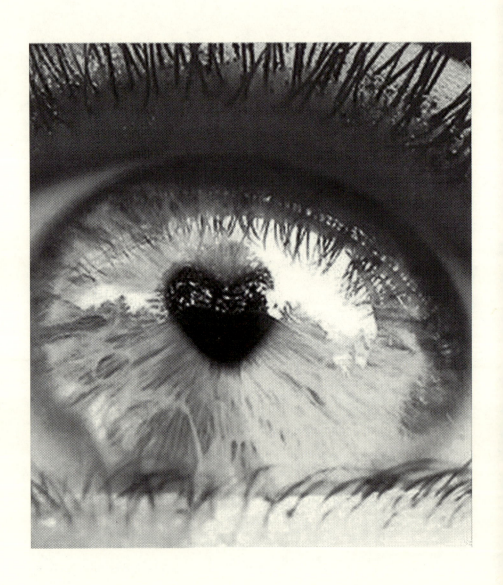

Believe Me

Believe me
When I lie to you;
Believe me, it doesn't matter
What you feel for me.

Believe me
When I pretend;
Believe me
It's not love I show,
But only friendship.

Believe me
When I turn away;
Believe me
At times of devastation
The love is true;
Nothing changes.

Believe me
When I say I must go;
Believe me,
I'll be there even when I'm gone.

Nuclear Arms

I am in trouble hanging high,
If I fall I'll surely die;
You reach out to rescue me,
Your nuclear arms let me fall free.

I go swimming in a lake,
Become capsized by a wake;
You sail beside me in your yacht,
Your nuclear arms can save me not.

While walking on a city street,
I stumble over my own feet;
A truck comes directly my way,
Your nuclear arms can't save the day.

I'm driving down a steep hill,
Having no problem until;
I see your car begin to roll,
Your nuclear arms had no control.

In my heart I pity you,
For saving others you cannot do;
Unless you control your destiny,
And set your nuclear arms free.

Misunderstandings

All on my own
I've waited patiently,
For you, my pride and joy;
My sense of dignity.

I've squandered time
By second-guessing you;
It's caused so much pain,
The hell I put you through.

Will you please make room
To forgive my ignorance?
My decisions were wrong,
Under the circumstances.

I will discover a way
To mend any grief;
Believe me when I say,
The hurt will be brief.

Disturbed Mind

I've an indrawn attempt
To discover some thought,
Of all the large worries
That have been brought,
Upon my disturbed
And emotional mind;
I have been left
With no time to unwind.

From little to greater
They all seem to haunt;
These worries inside me
I really don't want;
But little can be done
To turn them away;
I hope I can rid of them,
There must be a way.

All that I can wish for
Is an opening door,
To open much wider
Then ever before.
As soon as it opens
I will know so much new,
And then I may realize
Just what I can do.

Best of It

From light to dark,
From warm to cold;
I feast then starve,
Feel young then old.

From comfort to pain,
From ease to stress;
I'm rich then poor,
Have much then less.

From strong to weak,
From praise to scorn;
I'm fresh then stale,
Have zest then worn.

From happy to sad,
From great to small;
I wish what I had,
Was the best of it all.

Senseless Death

I saw an eagle flying high,
A mighty bird up in the sky;
Circling in search for prey,
As it would most any day.

It looked so mighty, in total control,
Not troubling a single soul;
And as I watched it fly around,
I heard a familiar sound.

Then I saw it plummet down,
Lifelessly it hit the ground;
Why it fell seemed to be,
So very much a mystery.

I gazed around over the land,
There stood a man, gun in his hand.
I realized then what had been done;
The eagle had been killed for fun.

Before the eagle found its prey,
It lost its life a senseless way;
As for the man that was standing there,
He turned and left without a care.

All We Are

We are like stars in the universe
Destined for a significant purpose;
To light each on our own,
To be peaceful and content,
To compliment and conquer,
Fall and fade away,
Each on our own path;
Under very little change.
We are one as the universe is one;
Limited to control,
Limited to knowledge,
Along with being limited to power,
And questioned as to importance.
Without the true light,
There is complete darkness;
For every dying piece of energy
Newness appears,
As the circle of time goes on,
And our circle of life goes on.

Unusual Rain

It's a hot summer day and here we lay,
Under clear blue skies with the sun in our eyes;
Shining so bright it gives off radiant light,
Then the wind gently blows and cloud cover grows.

In time raindrops fall which refreshes us all,
Then the rain subsides and the clouds clear the skies;
Then back comes the sun shining on everyone,
Which shines with a smile but only for a while.

We wait for the rain as it may return again,
Which we are happy to greet because of the heat;
But much to our surprise we see abnormal skies,
And thunder roar we have not heard before.

Through the clouds raindrops seep as skies start to weep,
And unusual rain falls as we hear nature's calls.
The calls are of pain from falling acid rain;
All the beauty around is destroyed on the ground.

Broken Hearts

In the days of loneliness,
Another feels a fatal kiss;
Sensing beyond a barren sky,
There is no need to justify.

Indecent forms become humane,
Forming one from two again;
Out of darkness appears light,
Letting newness retain flight.

From older days and actions neat,
Come ideas that will repeat;
Endless worries come and go,
In a natural overflow.

Out of crevices so thin,
Arise emotions from within;
Dreams of rainbows beautiful,
Are true to some but not to all.

Actions seem to deceive minds,
Thoughts appear of different kinds;
Deep end concentration starts,
Then appear the broken hearts.

Heat Stricken

I would never have dreamed to be trapped in this place,
All charred and blistered and red in the face.
Dreaming of water and finding no trace,
Wishing the swelter I could somehow erase.

The hot wind keeps blowing and twisting on by,
Leaving me helpless with dust in my eyes.
Blinded I stumble and continue to fry,
As the sweat drains my body, leaving me bone dry.

Forward I journey on blistered feet,
Limping and stumbling because I'm so weak.
I cannot go further as now my bones creak,
And sand pulls me under; I'm unable to retreat.

There seems no answer but only a prayer;
I am in a dungeon, I do not know where.
There's nothing I can do but ask for some care,
As I look to my Maker to end my despair.

Then after waiting much to my surprise,
My body is shaded from cloud-covered skies.
Rain starts descending and tears fill my eyes,
Someone has found me, God answered my cries.

Eden's Dreams

Eden's dreams fade gradually,
With the expansion of society;
Forests disappear each day,
Eden's dreams fade away.

With increasing population,
Becomes less and less land;
As expansion continues,
An end seems at hand.

Take the resources used each day,
Watch Eden's dreams fade away;
Keep on taking and never replace,
Destroy the earth's entire face.

Take care of things the best we can,
As uses, needs, and wants expand;
Conserve and care for all things seen,
Make a new start to Eden's dream.

Roadside Dreams

On a dark, dismal night,
With the rain pouring down;
I found myself walking,
Many miles out of town.

The lightning was flashing,
Every minute or two;
And my heart began pumping,
I knew not what to do.

There on the roadside,
I stood cold as can be;
When I saw car lights shining,
As it pulled up to me.

The door suddenly opened,
So I quickly jumped in;
I glanced at the driver,
His face bearing a grin.

"Where are you going?"
The man suddenly said;
"Up the road a short distance,
To the next town ahead."

The ride seemed a long one,
When it shouldn't have been;
Then everything darkened,
Nothing was to be seen.

Then before I knew it,
I was safe in my bed;
It appeared I was dreaming,
It was all in my head.

One that Got Away

Early in the morning we arrive at the pier,
Fill up the fishing boat, and throw it in gear.
Head out for deep water with big ocean swells;
The ride will be choppy but we will have pails.

The distance is a far one which will take some time,
But where we are headed the fishing is prime.
When we finally arrive we'll set up the rods;
Attach the downriggers and fish for the hogs.

It's a time to be patient, wait for the big strike;
You'll grab the rod handle, make sure the line's tight.
Then comes the feeling as blood runs through your veins;
Your heart will pump quickly when you have the reins.

Keep pulling and reeling, and feel your arms grow weak,
Then comes the magic moment, the big excitement peak;
Watching your trophy as it drags your line to the stern,
That catches up in the motor and suddenly you learn.
That was the big one that sadly got away,
But you might get a chance to catch it another day.

Lost Chance

I loved you more than anyone,
And wished I'd been with you;
You and I could have been one,
Making our dreams come true.

I longed to sweep you off your feet,
But now it was too late;
I didn't want to face defeat,
The pain would be too great.

I blamed myself for wasting time,
And for not making the move;
The moment may have been prime,
For us to grow in love.

When I had the will to care,
And give you all I could;
You were no longer standing there,
I did not expect you would.

If you read this please don't cry,
I was wrong to pass you by;
I realize it's too late to try,
To start my life with you.

Miss Me

Hold me now before I go,
Let the love you withhold show,
Speak to me, please let me know;
That you will always miss me.

Release your thoughts before I'm gone,
For I am not to live too long,
Sing to me that special song;
That you will always miss me.

Rid my soul of all my fear,
Which has always lingered near,
Tell me what I long to hear;
That you will always miss me.

When I'm gone and far away,
In your heart you'll feel me say,
I'll be with you every day;
You'll never have to miss me.

Day After Day

Day after day, night after night,
My thoughts of you, I continue to fight;
Day after day, night after night,
I look to pass by you if timing is right.

Day after day, night after night,
I hope to be with you with all my might;
Day after day, night after night,
I want to be near you, have you in my sight.

Day after day, night after night,
Seeing your face would give me new light;
Day after day, night after night,
I long to hear from you, wait for your invite.

Day after day, night after night,
I need your passion, it gives me such delight;
Day after day, night after night,
I wish to be with you and dream to unite.

The One for Me

The day I set my eyes on you,
I didn't realize what to do;
A light flashed brightly in my mind,
Which said you were one of a kind.

Yes, something said you were the one
To be around and have some fun.
I liked your laugh and loved your smile,
And knew being with you was worthwhile.

I didn't care what others said,
I told them I would go ahead;
I set my mind on you alone,
And wanted you for my very own.

Through my devotion I had received
More than I had ever believed;
The day would come when I'd marry you,
As I had always wished to do.

I hoped my dreams would all come true,
And they did when I met you.
How could I be so very lucky
To have you here beside me.

You're the One

You came from above
In just the right time.
I cherish your love,
Hoping you cherish mine.

You're a piece of my heart
That keeps me strong,
Which I cannot part
For very long.

Without you nearby
I become weak.
And that is why
Your closeness I seek.

I'm here for you
And will always be.
My love will be true
As you'll always see.
My heart will be yours
Whenever you need me.

Burning Desire

The fire burns before us
In a cabin very small;
Yet for some reason I am cold,
And feel no warmth at all.

Closer I snuggle to you,
As a solution for my concern;
Yet it seems to do no good,
As I am quick to learn.

Suddenly I begin to shiver,
So I move closer to the fire;
It suddenly envelops me,
Which was its true desire.

There you sit all by yourself,
Shocked by the circumstance;
Then tears of pain begin to fall,
As you take your last glance.

The raging fire in front of you
Is quenched from falling tears;
Amidst the smoldering embers,
The one you love appears.

You quickly reach out for me
With passion in your heart;
And we unite again as one,
Never wishing to be apart.

The Drifter

He had snake skin boots
And a hat of black felt
A long overcoat
And a bullet filled belt
A sleek six shooter
That he handled so neat
And shiny silver stirrups
Which clicked on his feet.

Over his chin
Was a half grown beard
Through his pale skin
Rough eyes peered
Around his neck
Was a disfigurement
From past encounters
At towns that he went.

He was a drifter
From places southwest
Most people knew of him
And what he did best
All men had realized
Why he'd been around
For when he disappeared
No law breaker was found.

Behind him was left
A blood shed trail
Of criminal men
Who escaped from jail
All of the duties
He wished to fulfill
Were all followed through
With pleasure and will.

The Game Of Golf

It's a sport people play,
Faithfully day after day;
Through the wind and the rain,
Which to some is insane.

With your club in your hand,
Hit the ball, watch it land;
Shooting straight as you can,
Will be your biggest plan.

Aim right at the pin,
And try to hit it in;
Count your strokes for each hole,
Taking few is your goal.

It's a game to enjoy,
For a girl or a boy;
If you start young or old,
You can learn quick I'm told.

It's something you can do,
With a group or just you;
When relaxed you play well,
Or get stressed, then it's hell.

If you swing and you miss,
Take some time to practice;
Maybe you'll like to play,
And be a pro some day.

My Hometown

I will ask you a question
About a place I know,
Surrounded by prairies
Where wheat fields grow;
A place on the flatlands
Where prairie winds blow,
That seldom sees heat waves
But often sees snow.

Have you heard of this city
In the middle of two,
Which is populated
By many people who
Are friendly and giving
And hard working too;
This city is such one
You've most likely been through.

You may ask me where I'd be
If I had my own way,
Most likely in this place
On any given day;
Why would I be here
You probably would say,
Because it's my hometown
The best place to stay.